AT YOUR SERVICE

Published by Spines
ISBN: 979-8-89383-493-2

AT YOUR SERVICE

REVISITING THE ANGELIC MINISTRY - HELP IS HERE!

KWASI ELI AMOUZOUVI

DEDICATION

Gratitude to my father, my best friend, Comi Pierre Amouzouvi, and my late mother, my very good friend, Mawuko Marcelline Assignon-Amouzouvi.

Special dedication to my son, Koffi Eli Amouzouvi.

CONTENTS

FOREWORD

In the journey of life, amidst its myriad complexities and challenges, we often seek guidance, comfort, and assurance. It is within the pages of this profound work that we embark on a transformative exploration of spiritual truths, anchored in the divine wisdom of scripture.

The author skillfully navigates the depths of spiritual understanding, weaving together profound insights with practical applications. Through intricate parallels drawn between the tangible world and the ethereal realm, the reader is invited to contemplate the mysteries of existence and the profound role of divine intervention in shaping our lives.

With meticulous attention to detail, the author elucidates the ministries of angels, illuminating their significance as celestial beings entrusted with the task of safeguarding, guiding, and uplifting humanity. Drawing from a rich tapestry of biblical narratives and contemporary anecdotes, this book serves as a beacon of hope and enlightenment for those navigating the vicissitudes of life.

As we delve into the intricacies of spiritual stewardship and divine intervention, we are reminded of our inherent connection to the sacred and the profound impact of aligning our lives with divine purpose. Through fervent prayer, unwavering faith, and a deep understanding of spiritual principles, we are empowered to transcend earthly limitations and embrace the fullness of our spiritual potential.

In a world fraught with uncertainty and turmoil, this book stands as a testament to the enduring power of faith, resilience, and divine grace. It is a heartfelt invitation to embark on a journey of spiritual discovery, where the presence of angels becomes palpable and the guiding hand of the divine leads us ever closer to our ultimate destiny.

May the insights contained within these pages serve as a source of inspiration, solace, and empowerment, guiding you on a transformative journey towards spiritual enlightenment and divine fulfillment.

INTRODUCTION

The servant of the man of God got up early and went out, and behold, there was an army with horses and chariots encircling the city. Elisha's servant said to him, "Oh no, my master! What are we to do?" Elisha answered, "Do not be afraid, for those who are with us are more than those who are with them." Then Elisha prayed and said, *"Lord, please, open his eyes that he may see."* And the Lord opened the *servants' eyes and he saw; and behold, the mountain was full of horses and chariots of fire surrounding Elisha.* 2 Kings 6.15 -17 (NIV)

This record shows a revelation inaccessible to the servant, yet visible to Elisha. Surrounded by a legion of foes, and demonic forces, what do you see? What you see will surely determine the next phase of your battle, either punctuated with sorrows, mourning, unrest or confidence, rest, and peace. Those bringing peace are God's angels made available to those who are to inherit salvation. Friends, who and what is challenging you, and who's on your side to defend you?

It stands to point out the ever-growing need for help to those who are 'to inherit salvation', in a troubled, brutal, and ruthless world. In a spirit-controlled universe, from decision-making to prayer warfare, choice of relationships, etc... those destined to salvation need deeper understandings, resolve, and clarity of rules of engagements, in seeking, experiencing, and fully enjoying the privileges inherent to their identity. The help isn't for all but designed for a category of people: the redeemed of the Lord, according to Psalms 107.2. In fact, the book of John outlines with clarity, the nature of those individuals, as it's written: *'Yet to all who received Him, He gave the power to become sons of God, to those who believed in His name'* (John 1.12). 2 Kings 6:15-17Amplified Bible (AMP)

Believers in Christ know about God the Father, the Son, & The Holy Spirit. Sadly, the church seems to lack understanding of God's angels and their very important roles in the Christian communities. Controversies, over the years, made it difficult for many denominations to embrace, teach, and summon angels for assistance in their dire situations. If it's imperative to remind us all that angels are not to be worshipped, praised, or venerated, --- '...angels are only servants--spirits sent to care for people who will inherit salvation' [New Living Translation]--- these beautiful beings are somehow 'hanging unemployed'. But how can they be employed if those they are destined for ignore them, and barely find a place for them in their prayer rooms? How to remediate such unfortunate reality, and make efficient use of this tremendous help God had lavished his children with?

WHO ARE THESE BEINGS CALLED GOD'S ANGELS?

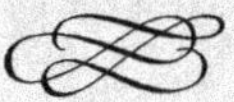

Please note that there are demonic angels, but we have no time to elaborate on them, as they're commonly called demons and archdemons So, God's archangels and angels are '... *ministering spirits sent out [by God] to serve (accompany, protect) those who will inherit salvation'* according to the [Amplified Bible (AMP)]. In this vein, it's crystal clear that for salvation to be sustained, help is needed from God's angels. The knowledge of the ministry performed by the angels is key to understanding God's full provision to His people thru Christ Jesus; it's critical to fully apprehend the very core mission of these beings called angels, made specifically to help us, not from time to time, but daily. The body of Christ has everything to gain in revisiting the angelic support she's destined to enjoy in good times and bad.

This is not a mere wish, but a strong reminder to the church that salvation is coded to success thru angelic help; to grasp it is to enjoy the full scope of our destinies, as both individuals and communities.

Apostle Paul asked the Corinthians if they had received the Holy Spirit. They answered 'No', and added: 'we have not even heard that there is a Holy Spirit'. Paul inquired further of the nature of the baptism they received and the Corinthians replied: 'John's baptism'. The Apostle told them: 'John's baptism was a baptism of repentance. He told the people to believe in the one coming after him, that is, in Jesus' As a result, 'they were baptized in the name of the Lord Jesus. When Paul placed his hands on them, the Holy Spirit came on them, and they spoke in tongues and prophesied.' according to Acts 19. 1-6. This account resembles that of us who either ignore the very role of the angels or have a misty concept of them. We are told and read about the angel Gabriel so much that we limit, oftentimes, the roles angels play in delivering messages, divine messages. It's paramount to invest time in elucidating the quantitative and qualitative roles played by these servants.

QUANTITATIVE MISSIONS OF GOD'S ANGELS

Who could provide better intelligence on the number of celestial hosts at Jesus' disposal during His earthly ministry, other than Jesus Himself? He evoked in Matthew 26. 53: *'Do you think I cannot call on my Father, and he will at once put at my disposal more than twelve legions of angels*? [New International Version] He made no mystery of the reason beyond his defenselessness and the impossibility for them to be deployed on that very day in the garden of Gethsemane; verse 54 shed more light: *'But how then would the Scriptures be fulfilled that say it must happen in this way?'*

It's worth noting that in those days, a legion represented about 5000 to 6000 men in the roman army. Jesus referred to 50,000 to 60,000 and more men to come to his rescue, should he need them. To mention such a large number of angels for His defense reminds us of his early days in the Ministry. Through divine illumination, we now understand how Jesus drove *'out [with force] the people who were selling and buying [animals for sacrifice] in the temple area, and overturned the tables of the moneychangers [who made a profit exchanging foreign money for temple coinage] and the seats of those who were selling doves'*; Jesus *'would not permit anyone to carry merchandise or household wares through the temple* [grounds, using the temple area irreverently as a shortcut]' Mark 11. 15-16 [Amplified Bible (AMP)]

Under no circumstances, would Jesus exert such a 'forceful action' against the traders inside the Temple by His own physical strength. Divine illumination helps us understand that the temple administrators allowed traders to do business on its grounds, levying taxes to support temple operations. Hence, these traders were valuable people in society, noble individuals; let's not forget the bodyguards at their disposal for security purposes. Mighty men guarded the Temple grounds and the wealthy did business successfully with approval from the High priests. Parallel to these strong dudes, deployed to secure and guard people and goods, Yeshua, whose physical traits are described as *'a young plant, and like a root out of dry ground; he had no form or majesty that we should look at him, and no beauty that we should desire him'* in Isaiah 53. 2 [English Standard

Version] couldn't have impressed them, to the point of chasing them out of the temple and worse, resist folks 'carry[ing] merchandise or household wares through the temple.' This specific occurrence should be a flashpoint for recognizing the quantitative role played by the legions He mentioned in the garden of Gethsemane. They overwhelmed those in attendance on that day of rage. Under normal circumstances, Yeshua would have been confronted, beaten, and worse thrown into prison. No one dared resist Him; they took off and fled the scene. Who knows if some felt something hit them hard, as they tried to stand their ground? I received no illumination on that, just a fertile imagination. Let's remember that there are many unspoken mysteries, just like the Scriptures never mentioned Isaac complaining to his mother over the attempted murder Patriarch Abraham almost carried out.

According to God's perfect plan, Jesus had to act to prevent corruption, lies, and all sorts of impurity in God's very Temple and set up an example for His people. Doesn't he Bible honorably refer to our bodies as the Temple of God? *'Don't you know that you yourselves are God's temple and that God's Spirit dwells in your midst?'* asks 1 Corinthians 3. 16. Can we today, the body of Christ, pretend to put order in our lives without the help of the legion of heavenly angels? Are we able to witness the growth of the church without deploying them? Can our marriages hold strong without the ministry of these beings? It's a question we need to answer first individually, then collectively. It appears clearly that Jesus acted to purify the Temple with tremendous help from the legions of angels from his Father. He couldn't have done it with a human hand. Hosts of Mighty and fearsome beings were sent to help Jesus, the Captain of our salvation, so should our battles be, our struggles be, and our actions be rescued by angelic support. Like any buildings or temples, angels are to guard our doors and gates; gates of our lives, doors of our minds, hearts, mouths, and sexual drive. To bring captive thoughts of fornication, adultery, and sexual immorality, angels are made to help you and me, not just our ability to pray or speak in tongues, not even the anointing, as these particular defilements seem, at times, to disregard anointing. Angelic guardianship is indispensable in aspiring to live a life of sanctification and consecration.

Mighty angels of God have intervened and helped human beings throughout millenniums. Records of phenomenal events indicate how angels brought victory to the people of God. Referring to them as 'mighty men', an account of wars fought by David's military cohort still impresses to date, though most of us ignore the real substance of these events which brought immense Glory to God in the sight of Israel and their enemies in the old testament. Adino, the Eznite, on one occasion, slew eight hundred enemies. Eleazar stood up and struck down the Philistines until his hand was weary and clung to the sword. Abishai the brother of Joab the son of Zeruiah wielded his spear against three hundred men and killed them etc... record found in 2 Samuel 23. It's obvious that not a single man on earth, except for the use of a weapon of mass destruction (WMD) has the ability to wield a spear and slaughtering 300, 800 men at once... More quantitative instances have been pinpointed by the Scriptures, where the angels guaranteed victory to the people of God before their enemies.

Asa called out to the Lord his God and said, *"Lord, only you can help weak people against those who are strong! Help us, Lord our God! We depend on you. We fight against this large army in your name. Lord, you are our God! Don't let anyone defeat you!"* [2 Chronicles 14:11 Easy-to-Read Version (ERV) Sent forth to 'help' the Israelites, the people destined to 'win the battle' by ricochet 'inherit salvation', the legion of angels defeated the Ethiopian armies. Let's remind ourselves of the numerically disadvantageous number of the Israelites –580,000 men--- compared to the astronomical number of men and military equipment owned by the enemy ---over a million---, Zerah of Ethiopia. Why do we refer to the legion of angels? One may ask. Wasn't it a strategic and tactical warfare fought by the Israelites that made them victorious? Though legitimate, the assertions lack truth, as verse 13 states: '... They were crushed by the Lord and his army'. Simply put, God intervened and dispatched the heaven hosts to defend His people. We too, can cry out, not because of righteousness, works, or merit, but because of the finished work of our Lord and Savior Jesus! The redeemed of the Lord are those who are to 'inherit salvation', and angelic help isn't optional, but the backbone of a happy and successful Christianity. Always remember that the flesh is weak and the spirit is strong. When evil forces challenge us, it's done from a weakness principle, as they know we are but, flesh; when we call on the Lord of all spirits, He sends down the legion of angels to our rescue. Asa confessed: *'Lord, only you can help weak people against those who are strong! Help us, Lord our God!'* Help can only come from the Lord of the helpers.

Through their forceful deeds, the quintessential role of the legion of angels is helping, assisting, defending, protecting, offending, and neutralizing threats, and shielding God's people, beloved, chosen, and anointed. I pray our tongues are untied, our lips unsealed, our hearts sensitive to cry out when cohorts of thousands, millions confront us, surprise us, oppress, and brutalize us; there is help available for us, the body of Christ.

What have we to say about the man with an unclean spirit whose dwelling was among the tombs? Held captive by strong and mighty unclean beings, *'no man could bind him, no, not with chains: because that he had been often bound with fetters and chains, and the chains had been plucked asunder by him and the fetters broken in pieces: neither could any man tame him.'* Mark 5. [King James Version (KJV)] Please note the indication: "...the chains had been plucked asunder by him ..." By him/ by her, that's how society, worse, the church qualifies, judges our behavior when overwhelmed by unclean forces, legions of destructive and savage spirits. However, the striking reaction displayed by the man, shows he was before a higher and superior detachment and authority. Why detachment? The possessed man, upon seeing Jesus, 'ran and worshipped him, cried with a loud voice, and said, what have I to do with thee, Jesus, thou Son of the Most High God? I adjure thee by God, that thou torment me not.' A deceitful statement to the human ear, as he did speak not in plural, but singular. How often do we consume fake reports produced by the devil? Fake medical reports about our kidneys and lungs, brain, spine, etc... and believe in those, without any insights from the legion of angels? Jesus quickly exposed the real story, as he interrogated the voice on their name: *'What is thy name?'* The unclean spirit answered, saying, *'My name is Legion: for we are many.'* A clear depiction of what the poor man was going through. Caught in a vise by 5 to 12 strong men, can one fight back, efficiently, unless endowed with a certain supernatural strength? Can one escape without being caught? This poor man has been held captive by 6000 strong men. Society calls his condition madness, or insanity; divine vocabulary identifies it as possession, demonic control, influence, and manifestation. Without versing into the broad aspect of this event, what made the unclean man step forward and worship Jesus? Remember Jesus, the skinny master in town; also, no one dared use the pathways to the cemetery where the possessed man used to live, for fear of being harmed.

Upon seeing Jesus, the Scriptures state that the demon-possessed *ran and worshipped*. In a military setting, that's a call to 'surrender'. What could make the legion surrender? Surely, the Anointing upon Jesus' life, but most importantly, the 60,000 + giants and fearsome cohorts. 6000 have no other option, but to prostrate and chant victory to the other camp. Beloved, we are the other camp, the camp of victors, the camp of those who should subdue, should be subdued, and have to subdue the world of darkness by the power in the Name of Jesus through the Holy Spirit by the help of the Mighty legion of angels. Demons will only manifest proactively upon seeing the children of God fully supported by the legions of angels. Demons are fallen angels and know what they are up against when the encounter occurs. They are no fools and know how to plead their cause when the circumstances are unfavorable. The church is full of contrary spirits and their numbers are increasing, because of the lack of understanding of the critical roles played by the angels. The Holy Spirt can inhabit us, yet the manifestation of angels will be limited, due to misunderstanding and misapprehension. Paul the Apostle stated by divine illumination: '...*how can they hear about him unless someone tells them*'. Romans 10:14-15 [New Living Translation (NLT)]. The time to tell is now.

Demons will bow, manifest upon seeing the legions of angels that surround us. Today, in some congregations, we see such occurrences, yet those who have no idea what the critical roles of angels are, label them demonic, fake power, etc... Of course, there are fake sources of powers out there, but not all; discerning spirits help identify the true from fake. Labeling miraculous signs performed by Jesus as that of Beelzebub doesn't make them so, rather, the awesomeness of God's mercy upon mankind unveiled. Do you know discerning spirits are angels as well? Would demons prostrate before Jesus when they see you? Would they negotiate their escape? Indeed, they will flee, prostrate, and negotiate, but the secret resides in the legion of angels following, backing you up.

I pray the legions of angels be deployed on our behalf, individually and collectively, so that the bride is made powerful, in Jesus' Name! Psalms 91.7 *For He will command His angels in regard to you, to protect and defend and guard you in all your ways* [of obedience and service].' [Amplified Bible (AMP)] Being protected, guarded, and defended demonic knees have to bow and tongues confess Jesus is Lord to The Glory of The Father when they face us.

Jesus rebuked the storm with a command: *be still!* Who was he talking to? Demonic beings stirred the water, as they knew He was on His way to free the man they held hostage for years in the tombs. The legion of angels showed up and crushed the resistance of these sea monsters. Quantitatively, they freed the passage and the boat made its way to the rescue operation scene.

Having spoken words full of audacity, Jesus faced an angry crowd. John 8. 59 gives an account of what could have been a death issue. '"*Very truly I tell you*," Jesus answered, "*before Abraham was born, I am!*" The reaction was almost immediate, violent, and fierce: '*At that point, they picked up stones to throw at him. But Jesus was hidden from them and left the Temple.*' Come to think of it, how does one hide from amongst a mob? Yet, Jesus did hide, which means he was either surrounded by the legion of angels or simply erased from the mob's visual sphere. If surrounded by the Mighty Legion of God, the mob stood no chance to throw a single piece of stone at the Messiah. We too, should enjoy similar benefits of angelic protection, both physically and spiritually. Jesus was simply protected, guarded, and defended by the legion of heavenly hosts. A story about Pastor Hagee reveals that God is still in the business of deploying angelic protection to those He chose. A gun was pointed at Pastor Hagee, but no shot was fired; how can a shot be fired, when the legion of angels neutralized the threat? In many instances, angelic protection saved thousands, if not millions of lives. Think of tragic accidents when dozens die, yet someone comes out unharmed. Think of hurricanes striking an entire city with a single house standing untouched. Think of dreams in which assailants surround you, yet you escape or overcome them. This is angelic protection made available to those who seek an understanding of the critical role played by the legion of heavenly angels.

QUALITATIVE MISSIONS OF GOD'S ANGELS

Does the body of Christ even realize how privileged she is? To have a legion of angels at our disposal is the best 24/7 help God endowed us with. Psalms 34. 7 stipulates; *'The angel[a] of the Lord encamps all around those who fear Him, and delivers them.'* This angel, in its singular form, reminds us of the guardian angel, we commonly refer to. It takes divine privilege to have one!

In their endeavors to retake a vital swath of lands from terrorist or rebellious organizations in Syria, military forces backed by Russian air power made tremendous progress in a matter of months; a breakthrough which was impossible for almost 4 years due to limited resources, lack of tactical and strategic approaches in the Syrian depleted army. The Syrian Arab army was known in the region as one of the best before the war;

yet wasn't on point to defeat on its own, a myriad of terrorist organizations. Many military men lost their lives, including innocent civilians, and millions went into exile because of the inability of the central power to protect and defend efficiently. A pastor is de facto the central authority in the church and lacking in resources and strategic readiness endangers the flocks in an egregious way. The church will end up experiencing death in series, miseries, divorces, and many more, for forces of darkness are raging fiercely to defeat the church. In this case, the number of terrorists or rebels as they are called from different angles is huge. The helpers won't be deploying many cohorts, but a handful of men and lots of equipment to deal with the threat and crisis. The quality will prevail over the quantity.

We read in theguardian.com:' Syria's army and allied fighters, backed by Russian air support, have been advancing towards Deir ez-Zor on several fronts in recent weeks, and on Tuesday arrived inside the Brigade 137 base on the city's western edge.' And 'This great achievement is a strategic shift in the war on terror and confirms the ability of the Syrian Arab army and its allies," the army command was quoted as saying.' [Tuesday 5 September 2017 11.02 EDT] The word 'strategic shift' remembers us of a transition from a chaotic initial state of affairs to a better one, as the army command stated: '...is a strategic shift in the war on terror...' Besieged on all sides, terrified by the multiplicity and sophistication of the multifaceted attacks on his troops, and on the verge of collapsing, the seating President called upon his helper, whose advanced technologies in warfare, well-trained military men, commandos, and experts could be of tremendous assistance. npr.org wrote: 'The Russian military involvement follows a request from [the Syrian President] to the [Russian President], according to Syria's state news agency, which reports that the President asked for Russia's intervention in a letter that cited Russia's efforts to fight terrorism.'[September 30, 2015, 8:37 AM ET]

To be involved, the angels are to be let in. Let's not forget that our prayers for angelic support are a 'request' and their support is 'assistance', a help. When the head of Syria called, an analogy of leaders ---fathers in the house, pastors in the church, or simply individuals on their own--- the Head of Russia responded, an analogy of God Almighty who answers our request. Russian Spetsnaz, the Elite forces, commandos, along with the most sophisticated equipment, ranging from fighter jets to radars and anti-missile defense systems were sent forth, a similitude with angelic deployment, along with their expertise and deadly force. Within months, a shift occurred, helping the Syrian government regain tremendous vital points in the homeland. This illustration is deemed relevant to help the reader apprehend the full scope of what God has made available to His people. Refugees, in the thousands, returned home as a result of the 'shift' operated by the intervention of the helpers.

In no way, can a mere mortal be compared to God Almighty, nor their fugacious deeds to His Eternal works. Let this be clear!

What difficulty are you in? How dire are your circumstances? Who's stealing your peace and vowing to bring you down? Do you realize the immensity of defense and security forces at your disposal? All you have to do is to call on the Head of the legion of angels; forward your request thru prayer and petition with thanksgiving, and continue to make your [specific] requests known to God. Philippians reminds us: *'Do not be anxious or worried about anything, but in everything [every circumstance and situation] by prayer and petition with thanksgiving, continue to make your [specific] requests known to God. 4.6 [Amplified Bible (AMP)].* These provisions are made available so the body of Christ knows the exact address where to forward her request for a timely rescue operation. Let's allow the Holy Spirit to lead us in prayers and invocations; soon the people of God will find themselves making 'specific requests known to God, as He alone knows what is best for us and the speed at which the specific request will be delivered. There is tremendous power in praying according to Spirit intimation; it creates room for the Holy Spirit and the angels to work swiftly on our behalf. The Holy Spirit delivers messages received from Christ and executed by the angels, so the Name Jesus isn't just a sort of 'first name' stuff, but God's Glory, Power deployed, Divine Decree Established, Oracle Pronounced & Manifested.

The Head of Syria knew exactly where to turn. He did not go around seeking help, for the odds of being turned down by weaker parties or enemies were beyond conceived limits. He sent a letter, though late, he remembers a sure ally, reliable friend, and partner. Do you, beloved in Christ, know you and I have more than a sure ally, reliable friend, and partner in Jesus? This reminds me of a hymn that never goes out of date.

What a Friend we have in Jesus,
All our sins and griefs to bear!
What a privilege to carry
Everything to God in prayer!
O what peace we often forfeit,
O what needless pain we bear,
All because we do not carry
Everything to God in prayer!

Have we trials and temptations?
Is there trouble anywhere?
We should never be discouraged,
Take it to the Lord in prayer.
Can we find a friend so faithful
Who will all our sorrows share?
Jesus knows our every weakness,
Take it to the Lord in prayer.

Are we weak and heavy-laden,
Cumbered with a load of care?
Precious Savior, still our refuge—
Take it to the Lord in prayer;
Do thy friends despise, forsake thee?
Take it to the Lord in prayer;
In His arms, He'll take and shield thee,
Thou wilt find a solace there

These verses speak volumes of the need for a reliable friend, ally, and partner. In real life, choose your friends wisely; a single one is enough if they meet the criterion of a reliable and true friend. '*The righteous choose their friends carefully....*' Proverbs 12:26 [New International Version (NIV)]. Every line of this hymn tells to what a true friend really is.

In accordance with the nature of the help sought, the S-400, S-300, the Pantsir, drones, and diverse warplanes literally changed the games on the ground. Devastation took over those fighting the Syrian armies, ruthless bombing from the 'helpers' and de facto annihilation of their fighting capabilities became obvious. The 'helpers' crippled the enemies' machinery, cut off supply routes, bombed weapon storehouses, and neutralized ground resistance with incredible airpower while scattering brutal reinforcement and reinforcing capabilities. Strategic government facilities and statehood symbols have been guarded. The Psalmist enjoyed such protection in the past: '*He strengthens the bars of your gates...* ' 147:13 [New International Version (NIV)]. The angels do more and exceedingly than those human tactics on our behalf.

Predictions to see the government and his Head fall or worse eliminated failed miserably. Rather words such as 'prop up' 'embolden' and the like took over reports about the man so many pundits predicted would be washed away by the movements he was combatting. Thanks to his helpers, the desperate man, slowly but surely, is bouncing back. How precious the help of a true and reliable friend! How vital their rescue! Folks, let's make no mistake. If this illustration of mere mortals lending a helping hand can shift in historic proportions the fate and destiny of a nation, how much more is our Father in the heavens with His legions of angels?

Remember, the presence of the angels does not always prevent all and every attack, as the Lord permits them to occur. Two main reasons behind these permissive measures: 1- to appreciate the value of God's marvelous plan to have helpers on behalf of His own. 2- to help us to enjoy the proceeds of angelic protection. Strikes from in and outside may come and cause discomfort, but the course to out victory is set.

Should we wait for disaster to come to seek help? Not at all! Disasters can be deadly and those who die lose their testimonies forever. In the medical world, research is ongoing to provide human kind with preventive measures due to the countless diseases which exist and confront the billions. In centuries past, a single ailment decimated entire communities; plagues suffocated vast populations and eliminated them. In dictionary.com, vaccine means 'any preparation used as a preventive inoculation to confer immunity against a specific disease, usually employing an innocuous form of the disease agent, as killed or weakened bacteria or viruses, to stimulate antibody production.' The Tech world identifies vaccines as a software program that helps to protect against computer viruses, by detecting them and warning the user.

Friends, we too, can receive preventively inoculation to confer immunity against specific diseases, plagues, turmoil, misfortunes, sudden death, incurable ailments, bankruptcy, and evil plans. We too, can enjoy a territory of joy and security, where, though struck, the arrows of the enemies are weakened before landing. It's more than a guarantee that we too, can be shielded, and protected against viruses by early detection and warning systems. Remember, advanced-knowledge is Power, Safety, and Peace. Legions of angels are ready to be deployed, for crisis-prevention. Send your request to the Head of the legion of Angels in Jesus' Name, now! Prevention is always better than cure, as when hit, we may lose venues to call on our helpers to intervene. If to cure means;' a means of healing or restoring to health; remedy, a method or course of remedial treatment, as for disease, successful remedial treatment; restoration to health', all hope is not lost. If curing means a successful remedial treatment and restoration to health, let's not keep our mouths shut, but ever open to call on the release of help.

In light of the progressive victories gained, thanks to the Russian army and while the war has not yet ended, we read in an Israeli newspaper Haaretz: 'Syria has not turned out to be a quagmire for Russia, no rerun of Vietnam or Afghanistan.' Also: 'Ironically... Syria is a success story.' 'But now that the survival of the Assad regime has been ensured and the enclaves controlled by rebels and the Islamic State are shrinking, what next for Putin in Syria?' The newspaper asked. Who writes the rules and history book at the end of a war? The winner, I guess. That's how God rewrites our story and shines upon us His glory! [Anshel Pfeffer (Kiev) Sep 22, 2017, 8:44 AM]

A record of a healing case contained within Mathew 8. 8-13 shows us a qualitative action executed by the angels, upon Jesus's instruction. By divine illumination, we gather that God's angels, according to times and seasons, based upon the divine will, can whisper phrases, words, and utterances to human beings. The goal is simple: The Holy Spirit knows the heart of God and what operations are booked to be carried out. The angels, who are subdued to the Holy Spirit, are able to receive orders and pass them onto those who are 'to inherit salvation'. The centurion received utterances and awoke Jesus' compassion. Has the centurion seen some of the legions of angels accompanying Jesus? Why did he assert *'For I also am a man under authority, having soldiers under me? And I say to this one, 'Go,' and he goes; and to another, 'Come,' and he comes; and to my servant, 'Do this,' and he does it.'*"? Was he expecting Jesus to send those under His authority to his own servant? Did he see medical doctors dressed in their medical blouses? Why was he referring to authority, under authority, and orders? Must he have seen something others saw not? A deeper understanding of God's swift action on behalf of the sons of men is simply impressive, formidable, and shocking.

In the Temple, those who did run to and fro, have they seen something the Bible did not mention? Why run in the sight of such a skinny man? Scriptures gave precise physical attributes of our Lord, nothing to impress. Should the mighty and fearsome dudes in charge of security and protection of goods and people in the Temple flee so easily before the physically tiny master? A critical mind and spirit know by divine illumination that maybe there is more here than meets the eye. With reason, Jesus declared: *"I still have many things to tell you, but you can't bear them now. When the Spirit of truth comes, He will guide you into all the truth. For He will not speak on His own, but He will speak whatever He hears. He will also declare to you what is to come.'* Through divine illumination, a better and deeper understanding is given to His people to grasp the relationship the Eternal God has established between the spiritual the physical, and the material. Let us remind ourselves that there is another level of understanding called the deepest, so let's not be satisfied when we reach a deeper understanding.

Qualitative angelic ministries appear to be more than what we can imagine. Not only on behalf of the centurion but also the Greek woman, a Syrophoenician by birth. She called on Jesus, whose answer was sort of scathing: *'It isn't right to take the children's bread and throw it to their dogs'*. To be called a dog in the midst of seeking help isn't an easy slap. Full of mercy, and because she was to 'inherit salvation' probably, her daughter, first, and her family afterward, an angel was sent to give her utterances. Jesus had no other option but to rush an invincible messenger to rescue the daughter. His reply was: *'Because of this reply, you may go. The demon has gone out of your daughter.'* I pray we receive utterances to enjoy divine provisions in each and every situation. Angelic utterances pre-dispose us to enjoy benefits tied to our identity, sons and daughters of The Most High God!

Receiving divine utterances was the first step to deploying divine compassion. Remember, the Bible says that we don't know how to pray. Rom 8.26 *'In the same way, the Spirit helps us in our weakness. We do not know what we ought to pray for, but the Spirit himself intercedes for us through wordless groans.'* [New International Version] Again, a clear reminder of the weakness of the flesh. The Holy Spirit controls the legion of angels; hence give utterances to those who are destined to be saved. It's imperative to remember that we were destined to be saved even before being created. Ephesians testifies to it: *'...even as he chose us in him before the foundation of the world, that we should be holy and blameless before him. In love, he predestined us for adoption to himself as sons through Jesus Christ, according to the purpose of his will, to the praise of his glorious grace, with which he has blessed us in the Beloved.'* C1. 4-6 [English Standard Version]. He puts an emphasis on the nature of the endowment we are the object of in v3 *'Blessed be the God and Father of our Lord Jesus Christ, who has blessed us in Christ with every spiritual blessing in the heavenly places'*. These blessings are multifaceted.

Just like a superficial relationship yields superficial exchanges, deep ones create deep exchanges. Blessing, according to the Merriam-Webster dictionary, means Approval, or encouragement. Remember when Jesus said: *'For God the Father has placed His seal of approval upon Him'*? John 6:27 [New International Version] which means he was blessed! Let's not forget the appearance of Moses & Elijah on the mount of transfiguration to encourage Jesus in the critical hours before the passion. The Holy Spirit is the ultimate blessing to us; angels are a blessing to us as well. It's critical to understand this: The Holy Spirit leaves in us, and angels do not. They help us but do not dwell within us. The driving force of the believer in Christ is the Holy Spirit, also known as the Anointing. By divine illumination, we can equally state that anointing is bestowed upon us in terms of level.

Ezekiel 47 talks explicitly of the Water, as a symbol of the Holy Spirit and its level upon one's life. '*When the man went out toward the east with a measuring line in his hand, he measured a thousand cubits, and he led me through the water, water that was ankle-deep. Again he measured a thousand [cubits] and led me through the water, water that was knee-deep. Again he measured a thousand [cubits] and led me through the water, water reaching the hips. Again he measured a thousand [cubits]; and it was a river that I could not pass through, for the water had risen, enough water to swim in, a river that could not be crossed [by wading].*' [Amplified Bible (AMP) Obviously, the more anointing we get, the more angelic hosts we receive to help; after all, the greater the battle, the greater the means to fight it. Seeking more anointing is increasing angelic support. These 2 privileges are inseparable.

MINISTRIES THEY PERFORM

Michael the archangel disputed with the devil and argued about the body of Moses, he led the battle against the dragon when war broke out in heaven. When the angel Gabriel has been blocked by the prince of the kingdom of Persia to deliver the answers Daniel needed for the liberation of the chosen God, Michael came to help the message bearer be free. The voice of the archangel will resound upon Christ's return for the dead in Christ to rise. The compilation is from 1 Thessalonians 4:16, Daniel 10:13, Revelation 12:7, & Jude 1:9

The rescue operation isn't just limited to human beings, but also to angels. Gabriel got rescued by another angel. This leads to thinking of the ranking in the military. A minister of communication, as we can identify Gabriel, needs a commando operation to be free from a hostage situation. No hostage situation took place when the same angel went on to visit Maria, Jesus' mom, nor Zachariah, John the Baptist's dad. This is a situation that pushes to reason that there are categories of communications from the angels that will not encounter resistance and others that will. It may happen that our dreams get fuzzy or completely lost upon waking up. Angelic deployment can bring to our remembrance what Heavens tried to communicate to us. Some dreams are just clear as we wake up and remain so for a longtime, in understanding and recounting phases of it.

In a world of constant fights, injustice, and great oppressions of all sorts, spiritually and physically, if only the church can refocus its attention on the continuous battle and the urgency of winning them rightfully, based upon our identity: those who are called to salvation, great success over our enemies will be achieved, both spiritually & physically. Understanding the critical ministry performed by the angels offers limitless opportunities that individuals and the church can enjoy. From rescue missions to intelligence needed to function.

Governments get power and leverage over their adversaries and enemies only when they have advanced knowledge of their schemes and strengths. Advanced knowledge is intelligence, accurate and concise intelligence. Operation Entebbe and Orchard carried out by the state of Israel show how advantageous it is to subdue the enemies and neutralize their capacity for destruction. In both cases, targets were smashed and threats and immediate threats were wiped out. The killing of Osama Bin laden was a matter of intelligence, concise and accurate. The Navy Seals, who stormed the building in Abbottabad, eliminated the target they went in for. Success crowned these operations, for the pieces of intelligence were crystal clear. In this vein, in many instances, angels, often called the angel of the Lord, or the 'Lord' spoke to individuals in their dreams etc...

On the contrary, in 2002, the battle of Takur Ghar in southeastern Afghanistan was a total failure for the United States, as incomplete pieces of intelligence-led the platoons to land in the lion's den. Special Forces were killed on the spot. A fierce gun battle took over the mountaintop where, highly trained forces were 'extinct' by peasants, farmers, and jihadists ruthlessly. Highly trained dudes were eliminated ruthlessly by jihadists. The similarity is found in the church, where based on incomplete pieces of intelligence, ministers of the Gospel jump into casting out demons and laying hands. In the process, they get struck, humiliated, or killed. No one plays with spiritual matters from a position of weakness and goes unharmed. Ask the sons of Sceva and you'll be educated accordingly. Acts 19. 16:' *Then the man, in whom was the evil spirit, leaped on them and subdued [c]all of them and overpowered them so that they ran out of that house [in terror, stripped] naked and wounded. [Amplified Bible (AMP)]. It's foolishness to engage in casting out demons on the mere quotation of '... they shall cast out demons...'* without understanding that this was a provision, not a shield. Long for the anointing of The Spirit and your angelic support will increase.

Church leaders will have a clear diagnosis of issues presented to them before offering a cure. Pastors, apostles, prophets, etc... need clarity of diagnosis before applying a cure. Guess for a second that you go to the doctor's office in search of healing, and the physician starts injecting products that aren't aimed at eliminating the threat you face, for lack of a thorough diagnosis. In this instance, the patient may be harmed or worse, die. But in the spiritual realm, the physician usually gets harmed or killed, for provoking a force they can't put up with. Remember David who called on the Lord and said: '*Give attention to my cry, for I am brought very low; rescue me from my persecutors, or they are stronger than I.*' Psalm 142:6 [Amplified Bible (AMP)] A believer in Christ doesn't just ignore the strength of his enemies, for it's deadly. Recognizing your enemies' strength helps prepare for the battles ahead. Indeed, battles. Archbishop Duncan William from Ghana once stated ---to paraphrase---: *'Do you realize that from his birth to death, Jesus had no break from fighting demons?'* This is a deep statement if we consider the scope of our calling and the urgent need to have angels help us. Similarly, David fought battles upon battles. Salomon had no battle to fight, but to build the temple and enjoy 4 decades of peace within the borders of the kingdom. So, are we to enjoy the proceeds of what Jesus did, in conquering victory on our behalf? Isn't the Scriptures right when it declared *we fight not for victory, but in victory?*

Legions of angels were the backbone of the early church. *'...For though we walk in the flesh, we do not war after the flesh: (For the weapons of our warfare are not carnal, but mighty through God to the pulling down of strong holds;) Casting down imaginations, and every high thing that exalted itself against the knowledge of God, and bringing into captivity every thought to the obedience of Christ...'* 2 Corinthians 10:3-6 [King James Version (KJV)] By divine illumination, the 'WE' stands for more than the human beings ---the church--, because somewhere, we find a record in Hebrew 12. 1 *'Therefore, since we are surrounded by such a huge crowd of witnesses to the life of faith...'* Spiritual battles are fought efficiently with the backing of mighty angels. They are made to support the material world. They carry out God's eternal decrees both preventive and defensive. God's word is true, therefore, set to yield results according to His principles.

Salvation is a race set before us and those who are destined for it are racers. The church seems to fail to grasp the relevance of the legion of angels. They preach the Holy Spirit, yet forget about the agents that carry out Divine decrees. Multifaceted roles attributed to the angels throughout the Scriptures are not an option for believers to seek, but a daily request to present before the Throne of Grace. Deployments of the angels are usually launched by God in His infinite mercy and often times by our own request, invocations, and prayers to the Father. Getting the church up-to-speed to ask the Father to release His legion of angels, should be an urgency of our times.

ANGELIC RANKS & TASKS

The world is based on a system of things. The spiritual controls the physical without exception. It's God's will. With respect to the heavenly legion of angels, they exist in terms of specific tasks and ranks. The US and Russia hold the most prominent places when it comes to the largest and most powerful fighting forces in the world. We'll be elaborating on the equivalencies and relevancy of their tasks as related to the US, Russia, and other nations' military ranks: Army, Navy, Air Force, Marines, and Coast Guard to name a few.

The Army: Ranks & Tasks [The Military Legion Of Angels]

'The Army exists to serve the ... people, to defend ..., to protect vital ... interests, and to fulfill ... military responsibilities.' We read on military.com According to the site, the mission of the army 'is to provide necessary forces and capabilities to the Combatant Commanders in support of the National Security and Defense Strategies. The Army continues to provide Combatant Commanders with a wide range of forces and capabilities to prevail in the war...Friends, *'For our struggle is not against flesh and blood [contending only with physical opponents], but against the rulers, against the powers, against the world forces of this [present] darkness, against the spiritual forces of wickedness in the heavenly (supernatural) places.* Ephesians 6:12 [Amplified Bible (AMP)] Waging such wars requires means and resources. If wide ranges and forces are needed to provide combatant commanders in the physical realm, how much more do we need for contending not only with physical opponents but also spiritually ruthless and violent foes? We read further that their roles also include: 'defense, peacekeeping operation, security of our borders, operations, and equipment to counter the flow of illegal drugs'

So many critical missions are fulfilled by the Army, reminiscent of what the Angels are created to do. Nations' security, defense, and crisis prevention are a complex issue, and so are our lives; make no mistakes about it. Our limited understanding makes it difficult to grasp the depth of this complex subject on the legion of angels. Ever wondered why the Israelites won wars in unusual manners? They either win in few numbers against a horde of mighty and well-trained enemies; from Philistine to Egypt or by just blowing trumpets and singing songs of praise unto The Head of the legions of angels. An account in 2 Chronicles 20 reminds us of what God does when His people call on Him, as they face turmoil, adversity, and massive attacks from the enemy. We read: '...*the Moabites and the Ammonites, together with some of the Meunites, came to make war against Jehoshaphat. Then it was reported to Jehoshaphat, "A great multitude has come against you from beyond the [Dead] Sea, out of [a]Aram (Syria); and behold, they are in Hazazon-Tamar (that is, Engedi)'* An overwhelming, traumatizing, and frightening report to the king. Important to note how the attack was massive, coordinated, and set to be successful. Our enemies don't come to us expecting to fail but to succeed in whatever they ought to do. Their plans are concocted to surprise, frighten, shock, and destroy us. Also, there seems to be a network of evildoers gathered together to defeat Israel at all costs. Any other king would go nuts upon receiving such a scathing report of an imminent attack, especially if no intelligence reports provide them with advance knowledge. '*Then Jehoshaphat was afraid and set himself [determinedly, as his vital need] to seek the Lord; and he proclaimed a fast throughout all Judah.*' King Jehoshaphat's only contingency planning to counter attack was to summon for a fast and prayer. A request was sent up to the God of the Universe and He will answer. '*...Listen carefully, all [you people of] Judah, and you inhabitants of Jerusalem, and King Jehoshaphat. The Lord says this to you: 'Be not afraid or dismayed at this great multitude, for the battle is not yours, but God's. Go down against them tomorrow. Behold, they will come up by the ascent of Ziz, and you will find them at the end of the river valley, in front of the Wilderness of Jeruel. You need not fight in this battle; take your positions, stand and witness the salvation of the Lord who is with you, O Judah and Jerusalem. Do not fear or be dismayed; tomorrow go out against them, for the Lord is with you.*' When God is involved in our battles, it's no longer ours. What a great consolation to know that a war declared unto us, is no longer fought by us, but by our Helper? Someone in Nigeria can be inspired and sing: 'there is something that makes me come into your presence, my Helper' Indeed, we all can find something that brings us into God's presence. His angels begin to help when we enter

His Presence. A calm overtook those in attendance, the king first. There is peace in God's presence; isn't it?

'So they got up early in the morning and went out into the Wilderness of Tekoa; and as they went out, Jehoshaphat stood and said, "Hear me, O Judah, and you inhabitants of Jerusalem! Believe and trust in the Lord your God and you will be established (secure). Believe and trust in His prophets and succeed." The frightened King is now exhorting his people. We only give what we have. We can only share peace when we have it, love when it speaks within us, and calmness when it dwells from within. The Angels of the Lord whispered the rescue mission to the King, now the waters are calm.

Witness the deployment of the heavenly Army. *'When they began singing and praising, the Lord set ambushes against the sons of Ammon, Moab, and Mount Seir, who had come against Judah; so they were struck down [in defeat]. For the sons of Ammon and Moab [suspecting betrayal] rose up against the inhabitants of Mount Seir, completely destroying them; and when they had finished with the inhabitants of Seir, they helped to destroy one another.'* Self-destruction emerges from confusion, and the confusion is immense; mutual destruction is inevitable. Dwight Eisenhower, a US general during WWII used the same tactic in confusing Hitler and his minions. Thinking that the allied forces would land on point A, they ended up being deployed on point Z. Great was the confusion. The Normandy landing crushed ultimately the evil agenda promoted by Hitler.

We read: '*When [the men of] Judah came to the lookout tower of the wilderness, they looked toward the multitude, and behold, they were dead bodies lying on the ground, and no one had escaped.*' See the handy work of the legion of angels God sent down to punish those who plotted against His people. Friends, getting the angels involved means victory in our battles, struggles, and challenges thrown at us. Cease battling the nonsense in your life. We are told to fight battles that we keep on losing, simply because we either ignore the rules of engagement or overlook them. How many times have you tried giving up on that addition of adultery, smoking, fornication, sexual perversions, socially deviant behaviors, etc....? Aren't you tired of pressing on a lost battle? You do not have the strength to put up with that battle. You claim to have the Holy Spirit but still fail when those temptations come knocking on your door. Indeed, you have the Holy Spirit but miss involving the legions of angels in your battle. An inestimable host of angels called the Army unit is available to get involved. Again, the process is simple: Send up the request and get a response.

The US went into Iraq to topple the bassist regime and didn't even wait for full victory before taking out the oil. So, are we destined to take the enemies' goods? *'When Jehoshaphat and his people came to take their spoil, they found much among them, including equipment, garments, and valuable things which they took for themselves, more than they could carry away; so much that they spent three days gathering the spoil.'* In the US, 29 different grades constitute the army ranking in the US Army. The lowest is called 'none' and the highest 'General of The Army'. Imagine the hosts and Ranks with regard to God's own Army. Folks, somewhere there is a record: *'He said,'... No; rather I have come now as captain of the army of the Lord.'* Joshua 5. 14 [Amplified Bible (AMP)] Folks, God got an army, a formidable one, with a Captain. Note that, the Jericho battle needed no more than a Captain, should we maintain the equivalency with the US army. So, neither a major nor a General of the Army was needed to complete the task. Joshua counted on the best of the best in the Israeli army to carry out military operations ahead. Heavens needed just the captain and his cohorts. Our battles will be insignificant if we call on The Lord of the Army to send us support, help, and reinforcement. *'The Lord is the God of Armies; the Lord is his name.'* Hosea 12:5 [Christian Standard Bible (CSB)]

The Navy: Ranks & Tasks [The Naval Legion Of Angels]

Why do those destined for salvation need naval legions of angels? They control the waters and their wealth, to be clear, they control money. The time was up for Jesus to pay his taxes. He instructed Peter: '*...go to the sea and throw in a hook, and take the first fish that comes up; and when you open its mouth, you will find a shekel. Take it and give it to them [to pay the temple tax] for you and Me.*' Matthew 17:27 [Amplified Bible (AMP)] The understanding of this verse is the foundational truth of financial freedom destined to those destined for salvation and the naval legions of angels make it happen.

Most of us think of loans, banks, and savings accounts when we are in need of money, which is natural. Fortunately, Jesus has shown His people, how to get the necessary funds to help meet their needs. The marine world controls money, all the money. Why on earth would the Rabbi choose such an atypical location? The record in Revelations 16. 5:Â 'And I heard the angel of the waters say, Thou art righteous, O Lord, which art, and wast, and shalt be, because thou hast judged thus". There is an angel controlling and patrolling the waters. Somewhere, there is a documentation of God's purposes vs ours, God's knowledge vs ours: 'For My thoughts are not your thoughts, and My ways are not your ways,' says the Lord. "For as the heavens are higher than the earth, so are My ways higher than your ways, and My thoughts than your thoughts.' Isaiah 55:8-9New Life Version (NLV) Surely, God's thoughts are higher than ours, and so is His knowledge. It takes knowledge and power to give such an instruction; we, the redeemed of the Lord are to have such knowledge and power to manifest. Paul, the Apostle eloquently put it: *'The holy nation of God is not made up of words. It is made up of power.'* 1 Corinthians 4:20 New Life Version (NLV) Listening to Jesus, one may wonder, is He out of His mind to suggest that tax money be 'withdrawn' from the river? Not at a specific location, but any first-caught fish? It'll be realized quickly that there is Power backing the word spoken, the instruction given. Indeed, *'The kingdom of God is not a realm of grandiose talk; it is a realm of power'* 1 Corinthians 4:20 [The Voice (VOICE)]

Kingdoms are not based on grandiose talks or pompous declarations but on power and authority. Empires didn't get established by mere talks but by the demonstration of might. Jesus did do just that. As usual, the servants, and the helpers were prompt to provide the Master with what was needed. I can imagine a colony of different species lined up to obey The command of He who is called '...*Wonderful Counselor, Mighty God, Everlasting Father, Prince of Peace'* Isaiah 9:6 [New

International Version] Friends, the Wonderful Counselor just got us counseled: the money is under the waters and believing that Angels are deployed on our behalf, end financial struggles many churches are facing. The church has almost everything, from prayer warriors to prophecies and beautiful sermons on faith, power, and corollary, but lacks one thing: money. This lack has caused major negative shifts in our communities, the sermons fail to '... *correct ...warn* ...' [2 Timothy 4:2 Amplified Bible (AMP)] as leaders are afraid to lose the tithes and offerings.

There is a 'Fleet Admiral' [United States Navy], on the waters, waiting to lead naval legions of angels to shift our financial situations. '*Then the angel whom I had seen standing on the sea and the land raised his right hand [to swear an oath]*' Revelation 10:4-5 [Amplified Bible (AMP)] He stands tall and invincible on both the waters and the earth. Feet stands for possession and possessing the treasures of the waters and those on the earth means total control over that which makes the riches of those '*destined to salvation*'. Why should possessors such as we the heirs and heiresses go broke? Isn't that curious, totally crazy? Indeed, until the soap is applied to the body, the skin remains filthy. Until we understand the rules of engagement to enter into possessions of the financial resources destined for us, the money will remain locked up, until proper request is sent forth for a release. Immense treasures are hidden under the waters for the people of God and never overlook the immensity of the waters. Oceans and seas combined make up 75% of the planet; 25% only is inhabited by mankind, animals, and vegetation. '90% of the world's merchandise trade now circulates at sea.' We read on rtl.fr [PUBLIÉ LE 27/10/2014 À 09:27 MIS À JOUR LE 27/10/2014 À 10:30]. This makes the waters, a serious business; the believer needs to seize upon. Isaiah 60. 5 reads: '*Then you will see and be radiant, your heart will throb and swell with delight; for the riches of the seas will be brought to you, the wealth of nations will come to you.*' [Complete Jewish Bible (CJB)]

'Oceans, the common heritage of mankind, play a central role in the organization and development of the world... The Navy therefore has the duty to control this space in its three dimensions (under the sea, on the sea, and above the sea) to preserve peace and defend our interests.' Excerpts from etremarin.fr To organize and develop require resources, enormous resources; simply put, financial means. The US developed, not just by human planning, engineering, and good management skills, but also by the cash flow, to the point of holding about 10 to 20 nations' military budget per annum. Impressive bridges and skyscrapers didn't just show up somewhere in Manhattan, Chicago, and Washington DC; money made them all happen. No matter how large and interesting your plans, your visions, your knowledge and understanding, no cash flow, no results. How then do we expect the church to have a tremendous impact in our communities, nations without the financial strength we need? Somewhere, the Scriptures tell us how eager the world awaits our manifestation' it's not just through our speaking in tongues, preaching, and sermons, but also, through visible impacts through financial means.

If human beings, with their limited knowledge and capabilities, thought wise to have an established force to defend the seas, not just floating on top, but to protect the bottom and defend it above, how much more the redeemed of the Lord? There is no way, one can really tap into the limitless resources the seas have in store, without the knowledge of it, the harnessing capabilities and to defend them at all costs. Who are the harnessers and the defenders?

Beloved, we, human beings, made in the likeness of God, are the harnessers, for this privilege has been given unto us at the creation. The wealth therein is plentiful and immense. 'The sea, a food to us all. Some impressive figures: 90 million tons of fish caught at sea each year. 65 million tons of fish and shellfish are raised each year ... The sea is essential to feed humanity's fremer.fr This demonstrates our huge dependency upon the seas and oceans. To make it happen, we need sailors and experts, equipment, hardware, etc...They are made to help us in the process and defend our perimeters.

To defend our perimeters, we need an Army, capable of maintaining a high level of security and defense capabilities. Understanding that we face adversity and giants, demands a readiness that can subdue the giants fighting, opposing, resisting, and at times defeating us in humiliating ways. The Navy is the military force that protects the seas, oceans, and waters in general. There is a massive naval legion of angels at our disposal. Remember, apply the soap, and the skin won't be filthy; in the same manner, send forth your request, redeemed of the Lord and you won't suffer defeat, brutality of misery, and poverty.

We read on Navy.com '... Navy is a necessary force and uncommon opportunity. There, to protect our country and to deter threats around the globe. There, to provide a challenging and rewarding future for those aspiring to pursue a bigger mission in life.' There could be no clearer explanation of the critical role played by the Navy.

France defined a new strategy, which means there was a previous one, that has been upgraded, so should our strategies, understanding, prayer life, etc.... France's new strategy is based on 5 functions:

- To Know and Anticipate

- To Prevent

- To Protect

- To React

- To Deter

The purpose of these pages isn't a food for thought notion, but to stir your spirit; it aims at pushing you into reclaiming what has always been yours, yet hijacked. I pray the Spirit of God 'stirs your spirit' as in the days of Samson, Gideon, and King Cyrus, so that you grasp the urgency of getting help from the legion of angels, especially, the naval legion of angels, in Jesus' Name!

1- To Know and Anticipate: To maintain our knowledge of the world and its functioning by monitoring and analyzing the world maritime situation, the Navy collects and disseminates maritime information for the benefit of the authorities. (etremarin.fr). Knowledge is power! Angels communicate knowledge, and educate on every and all aspects of life, according to Divine Grace. They do so, by monitoring and analyzing information collected on our behalf. Also, we read: 'Biodiversity, adaptability, resilience, acidification, warming, rising waters ... The ocean changes' on ifremer.fr which means that stock market, inflations, deflations, opportunities, and changes in opportunities are critical pieces of info we should be aware of way before any crash occurs, or any shifting happens.

We pray in Jesus' Name, that naval legions of angels work on our behalf, according to the Scriptures. Let them infuse us with critical financial pieces of information through dreams, visions, conversations and exchanges with strangers, etc...as it's written: '*I will instruct you and teach you in the way you should go; I will counsel you [who are willing to learn]...*' [Psalm 32:8 Amplified Bible (AMP)] Pieces of info that will help shift our financial status positively and drastically.

2- To Prevent: to act to avoid the emergence of crises that threaten our security. The Navy ensures permanent vigilance on all the seas of the globe. (etremarin.fr).

Prevention is better than cure. To keep crises and threats from hampering security is the best option anyone would prefer. How great to know that an established team is ready to keep menaces from affecting us. How refreshing to know an invisible and invincible team is ensuring permanent vigilance on our financial opportunities.

We pray in The Name of Jesus that the invincible naval team keeps us from evil, crises, and threats to our financial security, as it's written: '...*I will watch over you.' '[Psalm 32:8Amplified Bible (AMP)] You've promised Oh Lord, to keep me from all harm and watch over me*' Psalm 121:7 [New International Version]

3- To Protect: to guarantee the population against threats of every kind. The Navy contributes to the safety of seas and seamen through rescue missions, assistance to ships, surveillance of fisheries, anti-piracy, pollution, and drug trafficking.

Long before France defined this manual, a provision has been made available to the Redeemed of the Lord in 2 Thessalonians 3.3 '*But the Lord is faithful, and He will strengthen you [setting you on a firm foundation] and will protect and guard you from the evil one.*' [Amplified Bible (AMP)] Those in charge of protecting us are the legion of angels, in this case, with respect to our financial health, the naval legion of angels. He's promised, that all we do, is to 'remind' him by sending up a request for naval angelic support.

We pray in the Name of Jesus that while the naval angelic support is rooting for our protection and safety of our financial conditions, let the angels of '*discretion watch over us and that understanding and discernment guard us.*' Proverbs 2:11 [Amplified Bible (AMP)]

4- To React is to deploy our forces where necessary to restore peace, evacuate people at risk, or assist populations.

It's more than relevant to have peace restored to us and the first place where it is needed is in our mind. Peace can only be restored by actions of intervention, as prevention won't always correct all misfortunes. Special Forces are usually needed to restore peace to troubled citizens and that's the mission assigned to the naval legion of angels. They are to be deployed by our earnest prayers to restore peace in our financial lives. We've had instances when peace evades our mind due to our inability to pay rent, mortgages, car notes, insurance, etc... Friends, let's make it clear that we are not talking of extreme wealth for everyone, as it won't just make sense, but the vital financial minimum needed for peace to be restored within our borders is a work done by the naval legions of angels. Angels are tasked to evacuate our 'waters', sources of financial good health from menacing winds. In this instance, it could be your business, your job, any conventional and/or unconventional source of riches, or benefactors; they are to be evacuated from hurricanes, storms, prisons, shackles, etc... for you and I to enjoy God's unending financial provisions.

In Jesus Name we pray and command a naval legion of angels to react to every and any menacing winds threatening peace within our financial perimeters by restoring financial peace. We deploy the wings of those angels to secure our sources of wealth from winds, storms, hurricanes, squalls, and their likes, '...*and the peace of God, which surpasses all understanding, will guard your hearts and minds in Christ Jesus.*' Philippians 4:7 Christian Standard Bible (CSB)

5- To Deter is to maintain permanently at sea a nuclear submarine launcher of missiles (SNLE) to make fear an absolute retaliation to anyone who would attack the vital interests of France.

No one dares to attack a nuclear power, as the retaliation could be mutually devastating. The AMD theory which prevailed during the Cold War, though fearsome, was and still is the cornerstone of national securities in the USA & Russia. The very idea that a nation possesses a nuclear arsenal makes it a great deterrent for other nations, nuclearized or not. Let's face it, we live in a world where the weaker gets crushed. There may be a universal declaration of human rights, but we don't have the same rights, no. The earlier you realize it, the better.

Consequently, having a strategic balance and even dominance over anti-financial prosperity demonic forces, especially against the people of God, demands a naval angelic deterrence.

In Jesus' Name, we pray for an angelic deterrence to uphold our financial provisions and gains in signifying clearly a deadly retaliation on attempts to block, defeat, or attack us. *'Save us, O God'* Psalm 69 [New American Standard Bible (NASB)] in Jesus Name!

The Air Force: Ranks & Tasks [The Aerospace Legion Of Angels]

'For we wrestle not against flesh and blood, but against principalities, against powers, against the rulers of the darkness of this world, against spiritual wickedness in high places.' Ephesians 6:12 [King James Version]

Wrestling against spiritual wickedness in high places requires high-place fighters. The legion of angels is tasked to fight those battles on our behalf as we command them so, according to the Grace we receive.

Anything that fights you from higher altitudes overpowers you, it's just a matter of time. They may not be stronger or more experienced; altitudes give them tremendous leverage over you. No wonder you keep on failing that battle. If I throw stones at you from a 5-story building, you'll likely get hit severally on-ground and

I'll be able to escape yours. I may be the dumbest, but still will defeat you. Sadly, wicked demonic forces aren't dumb, but experienced; they've been at this for millenniums, you need a greater force to help, it's called the Legion of Angels.

We read on military.com core missions carried out by the US Air Force. Bombing runs, Close Air Support (CAS) for on-the-ground missions, Jetfighter patrols to protect airports, strategic locations, etc., Airborne mapping & monitoring of targets, Maintenance of aerospace systems and planes, Base/embassy/airport/other security, In-flight refueling, Special rescue missions behind enemy lines, Medical service in impoverished areas, Food & supplies distribution around the world etc...

In a nutshell, we see the vital roles played by the Air Force. Bombing runs remind us that the legion of angels works in concordance and cooperation for successful operations. Just like spiritual wicked forces can hit from the air to halt an operation being successfully carried out on earth, so does the legion of angels. Dictionary.com defines a bombing run as 'the part of a bombing mission between the sighting of the target or its identification by electronic instruments and the release of the bombs. The air-to-ground missiles are ready to hit the wicked plans devised against us'

Friends, we can be assured that our heavenly hosts are ready to release bombs to defeat that which has been harassing us for so long. The blast is generally ruthless and irreversible. The fire is in our mouth and at our command, through faith in Jesus' Name, Jeremiah 5. 14 becomes manifest: '... *I am making My words in your mouth fire...*' New American Standard Bible (NASB) Friends, there is power in the mouth of those destined for salvation.

Again, Close Air Support (CAS) for on-the-ground missions is critical to prevailing at all costs. Fighting isn't just on the ground, but also underground. Remember, bunker busters? Indeed, there are depths our enemies won't allow us to reach to fight and win or be free. '*Out of the depths [of distress] I have cried to You, O Lord.*' Psalm 130 [Amplified Bible (AMP)] ... the CAS mission becomes, critical, crucial.

Jet fighter patrols to protect airports and strategic locations, remind us of possible hijacking of airports and the blockade that can ensue. If considered like a list of things, needs, and vital needs to be transported by a cargo, then the airport needs to be secured for take-offs and landings. The legion of Angels is expert in this; they've been at it for ages. Strategic locations can be our churches, prayer rooms, work, fields of evangelism, homes, etc... If unguarded, our prayer rooms could be destroyed by the wicked forces in high places, and us growing cold in prayer. If unpatrolled, our churches could either become the house of perversion, heresies, or simply empty. If unguarded, our evangelism fields to bring in more of the heirs and heiresses could go unvisited by the beautiful feet of those who spread the Good News! We need the Air Force to patrol and guard our perimeters.

The highly targeted missions the Air Force carries out show how critical roles they play. Remember that this is aimed at 'spiritual wickedness in high places' and this is no joke. The quality or state of being wicked is quintessential to being wicked. Dictionnary.com defines wickedness as extremely dangerous. Hence, we need all resources to prevail; glory to God, the Heavenly host of the Air Force got them all.

The prince of Persia operates in the High places and seizes answers to our prayers. A record shows *'At the beginning of your petitions an answer went out, and I have come to give it, for you are treasured by God'* The next chapter tells us what happened: *'But the prince of the Persian kingdom resisted me twenty-one days.'* A fierce battle will follow, as God's Air Force commandos clash with this evil force in the high place. *'Then Michael, one of the chief princes, came to help me because I was detained there with the king of Persia.'* Daniel 10:13 [New

International Version]. Literally taken, Michael intervened up in high places to make a way for Gabriel, so that Daniel gets the answer. Remember the Close Air Support (CAS), such a dynamic clearly depicts how engineered the system is in terms of rescue operation, both physical and spiritual. This is no joke. Daniel previously said: '*...I, Daniel, understood from the books...*' *Daniel 9.2* [Christian Standard Bible (CSB)] which means Angels of understanding have been at his service, helping, yet the answer to his request was to be brought by Gabriel; Michael will handle the CAS in order for the resistance to be broken, for the blockade to be torn.

Repeat, through Faith, in Christ: Let all resistances be broken by the intervention of the Close Air Angelic Support. Resistance in high places blocking answers to my marriage, job, business, finances, ministry, progress, breakthrough, and all God's spiritual, material, and health-related blessings be broken, dismantled, smashed, brought down, lifted, canceled, and cursed by divine curses in Jesus Name, according to Leviticus 26:30 '*I will destroy your high places, cut down your shrines*', thus high places resisting my destiny are no more in Jesus Name! We are all rescued from behind enemy lines by the Air Force Power of our Father, Jehovah, in Jesus' Name!

What of the Navy Seal, Delta Force of the USA, the Spetsnaz & Alpha Forces of Russia? These are brutal elite forces, regardless of sugarcoating by their respective government and or media. Special Forces kill in a special way, liberate captives in a special manner, and destroy with special tactics; everything they do is special by reason of their procedures. We read on southfront.org 'A 16-strong Spetsnaz team close to the front lines identified buildings occupied by the enemy, its defensive positions, armored vehicles, munitions dumps, travel routes...In a single day, the small team of Spetsnaz repelled four attacks. By the most modest estimates, there were about 300 of them.' These 300 men have something in common: 'And they were highly trained, -Daniil assures us. -Afterwards, when inspecting the damage, we realized the terrorists were very well-equipped. Imported uniforms, go-pro cameras on their heads, and expensive field medical kits. Some dark-skinned mercenaries among them. Local Syrians don't have the money for stuff like that. Moreover, they displayed serious training on the battlefield. Their weapons are not only Soviet and Chinese but also US and Israeli.' These terrible and wicked men aren't just from within, but from the outside as well. But outsiders can only get in by virtue of insiders letting them in or providing them with intelligence specifics. Redeemed of the Lord, the battles we face aren't a product of imagination, but a real survival context, only those awake win, more reason to understand the relevance of what it means to get your helpers alert.

Made of flesh and blood, we are often times subject to insufficiencies, lacks, and severe weaknesses. Our enemy knows it and demons directed at us aren't humans, but spirits. Hence they know when to come in and sabotage the beautiful plans of our lives. Keeping your mouth open and commending the legions of angels to be deployed isn't optional. Remember what the Bible talks of with respect to the enemy irrupting into our perimeters while we're asleep? *'But while everyone was sleeping, his enemy came and sowed weeds among the wheat, and went away.'* As a result, *'When the wheat sprouted and formed heads, then the weeds also appeared.'* Matthew 13:26-27 [New International Version] We often get shocked, when after a prophesy of goodness, happens to look perfectly opposite, when our sweet marriage turns out to be hell, when our monthly salary seems to go thru a hole we know nothing about, when our nice and considerate children are shown on TVs as rapists, criminals. Indeed, the enemy came in and sowed crime, divorce, debt, poverty, miscarriages, and all evil devices destined to monitor and abort our destinies. Then are we to say like these servants: *'The owner's servants came to him and said, 'Sir, didn't you sow good seed in your field? Where then did the weeds come from?"* Thanks to the answer provided to his servants, we know who is guilty: the enemy. He can use our neighbors, family members, and co-workers or operate directly to block, fight, and worse kill us. Thank God for strong provisions made available to those destined for salvation:

Let's pray and command the angelic support, defense, and offense in Jesus' Name!

Have you ever asked yourself what Jesus said during his unending nighttime prayers? Jesus Christ, the source of life, Power, Mighty God, etc... Did He have to? Was He trying to just convey a message or teach us a deeper understanding? We believe it was both. To invest time with the Father through His Spirit in Jesus' Name! Also, by divine illumination, to infuse us with the understanding that such communion is critical to obtaining continuous angelic support on our behalf to fulfill missions we have been given and ought to give an account for. So, to escape the terror of the enemy sowing sickness and diseases, angelic defense is a must and the request is sent by prayer, earnest prayers.

Provision, according to dictionary.com means: 'something provided; a measure or other means for meeting a need.' And our needs are to be met by those who have been destined to meet them: God's angels.

When a driver buys a car, fuel, for instance, is a provision. For the car to run smoothly, depending on the distance, the tank either has to be full or half full. However, a full tank is best, as one may get stuck in traffic and run low on gas; what's next? Many took the highways to escape IRMA, a major hurricane. About a million people got simultaneously on the road. In the tohubohu, many lacked the money to fill up their tanks, while others had it full; still, others had their tanks full, but also extra bottles full of gas, in case the mass exodus caused an unending traffic. We got 3 categories of people, and the question is which category was best prepared? The 3rd one obviously. How far one will go is determined by the amount of fuel in their vehicle. During the trip, some stopped to replenish their tanks, so should the life of the Redeemed of the Lord be time taken to pray and obtain more support. These are basic life demands, yet critical in the realm of the spirit to our very survival, critical to our growth, critical to our destinies.

To get in the legion of angels, one needs to put in abundant, not the multiplicity of words, loudness, and long hours, but quality time with The Spirit who Gives words of prayers, as He alone knows God's Heart. Daniel was thrown into the lions' den yet was unharmed. Special Forces responded. This is a man who added fuel, and huge quantity to his vehicle before facing the tohubohu of demonic traffic on the way of his worship. He prayed many times a day, in spite of his high-ranked position within the palace. As an advisor to the King, Dan could have usually evoked his busy schedule not to pray, yet was disciplined. Friends, Special Forces simply removed the 'beastly faculties off the lion's systems until the Redeemed of the Lord was brought out of the donjon. We have been thrown into donjon and immediately got devoured, bruised, wounded badly, or bleeding to the point of death. Each category comes with its own angelic support status. Those who got devoured instantly surely had at their disposal weak angels, of a non-ranking capacity; shocking right? Remember that there are rankings; it's more than a military system, way above anything you and I can think of. From the bruised ones to the badly wounded, and to those bleeding profusely to the point of death, we now understand the rules of engagement in our prayer life.

We read on nypost.com 'A sharpshooter killed a top ISIS executioner and three other jihadists with a single bullet from nearly a mile away — just seconds before the fiend was set to burn 12 hostages alive with a flamethrower, according to a new report..' It went on: 'The British Special Air Service marksman turned one of the most hated terrorists in Syria into a fireball by using a Barrett .50-caliber rifle to strike a fuel tank affixed to the jihadi's back, the UK's Daily Star reported Sunday. The pack exploded, killing the sadistic terrorist and three of his flunkies, who were supposed to film the execution, last month, the paper said' [September 11, 2016, | 5:00 pm] We've heard of family tragedies where an entire household gets killed instantly, butchered ruthlessly. You, as the head of your house, need a sharpshooter, a special air Service marksman to rescue you and yours. Understanding facts about how the system of things works is paramount to our peaceful stay on this earth. A sharpshooter will target those robbers, criminals; and assassins sent your way before they reach your destination. Their car either crashes or a mighty wind keeps them away; their assignment either gets revoked along with their means of execution, or their lives are taken out one way or the other if they are human entities. Eternal chains either get thrown at the suckers or they are instructed to keep away from you if they are of a spirit nature.

KNOWLEDGE & UNDERSTANDING

On dictionary.com knowledge is defined as 'acquaintance with facts, truths, or principles, as from study or investigation'; on Merriam-Webster.com understanding is the power of comprehending, the superior power of discernment, enlightened intelligence.

Based on these 2 meanings, we can all admit to having knowledge of angels, through reading, and movies. We all know of Angel Gabriel for having brought the good news to Mary, Zachariah, and Daniel. We all know of angels attending Joseph in his despair etc... but most of us lack understanding of their roles and missions. The Power to comprehend, the superior power of discernment, the enlightened intelligence are the recipe for understanding, be it in sciences, or technologies.

Just like many have knowledge of many Apps, but lack understanding of their nature and practical use, so is our lack of these unique beings, destined to help heirs and heiresses of salvation. Now, what's salvation?

On Merriam-webster.com we read: 'deliverance from the power and effects of sin, the agent or means that effects salvation, liberation from ignorance or illusion, preservation from destruction or failure, deliverance from danger or difficulty'.

On dictionary.com, it's defined as 'the act of saving or protecting from harm, risk, loss, destruction, etc. the state of being saved or protected from harm, risk, etc., a source, cause, or means of being saved or protected from harm, risk, etc. Special note: 'In Theology: deliverance from the power and penalty of sin; redemption.'

According to cambridge.org salvation means '(a way of) being saved from danger, loss, or harm' with a special note: In the Christian religion, the salvation of a person or their spirit is the state of being saved from evil and its effects by the death of Jesus on a cross.

On biblestudytools.com salvation is 'Of the many Hebrew words used to signify salvation, yasa [[;v"y] (to save, help in distress, rescue, deliver, set free)' We read: 'Broadly speaking, one might say that salvation is the overriding theme of the entire Bible. But since it is a multidimensional theme with a wide range of meanings, simple definitions are impossible' More interestingly, it adds: 'The Old Testament. In general, the Old Testament writers see salvation as a reality more physical than spiritual, more social than individual ...The New Testament. The advent name "Immanuel, " "God with us, " signifies momentous progress in the history of salvation. In Matthew's Gospel, the angel tells Joseph that Mary's child is conceived of the Holy Spirit and that he is "to give him the name Jesus because he will save his people from their sins' Then, more light appears: 'The name "Jesus" (derived from the Hebrew Joshua [;[Wv/hy]) itself means salvation'

Let's remind ourselves of Hebrews 1. 14: *Are not all angels ministering spirits sent to serve those who will inherit salvation?'* [New International Version (NIV)] Deliverance from the power of sins, liberation from ignorance or illusion, preservation from destruction and or failure, and deliverance from danger or difficulty is to be saved. The means and or agents for that purpose is the legion of angels. Psalms 107 is utterly clear on the nature of men, and our conditions which ultimately begs for salvation. We read: *'Some wandered in desert wastelands, hungry and thirsty; their lives ebbed away'* also, *'Some sat in darkness, in utter darkness, prisoners suffering in iron chains, Some became fools through their rebellious ways, and suffered affliction because of their iniquities, They loathed all food and drew near the gates of death'* Time and again, the lines of this evoking Psalm depict our true nature, both physically and spiritually, yet the spiritual aspect is the most dire one. Physically, plagues, diseases, and hardships are devastating and unbearable; those abnormal occurrences are visible and palpable to us, our close friends and family members, yet we totally ignore and are unknowing of the spiritual devastation, our spiritual sorrowfulness, as the state of our spirits is the pure reflection of our physical nature.

The harlot freed from his past life, has surely never prayed for her own salvation; this usually occurs and we hear testimony such as; I just felt something leaving me, I felt a peace of heart, tears were gushing out of my eyes, I felt this life wasn't for me. An heiress to salvation just got 'served'. Angelic ministration goes beyond our understanding. Under such circumstances, the Holy Spirit who is the Overseer of the Legion of Angels, instructs, as per what He hears from Christ Jesus, that it's time to rescue Juliet, Donald, Sergey, Pablo, etc... No matter the locations, the darkness, executioners must carry out the rescue mission and secure the heir and or heiress spirit and soul. These are highly ranked and mighty legions of angels.

The believer in Christ, the brother highly involved in church activities needs the same angelic support to stand and enjoy his salvation. The brother is experiencing some addictions, he'll cry out for help. A testimony will follow. An heir just got 'served'. We see, again and again, the intervention of the legion of angels. It's real, manifest, and glorious.

The legion of angels protects us from harm, risk, and danger. With reason, Scriptures say: '*The [a]angel of the Lord encamps around those who fear Him [with awe-inspired reverence and worship Him with obedience], And He rescues [each of] them*' Psalm 34:7-9 [Amplified Bible (AMP)] Remember that these are benefits of being an heir/heiress to salvation. Friends, we enjoy angelic ministration each and every day without even realizing it. We have knowledge of them but still lack understanding of them.

Angels, as we mentioned previously, come in rankings, from none to Generals, and fulfill diverse missions. They are a plethora of beings, sometimes having a human form, bird-like shape. They can be sweet and brutal. In light of what the army constitutes, the angels are equally established to carry out their missions, when called upon, when the time is up to assist and apply God's judgments, sentences, and condemnation. They draw favor to us, cancel penalties, and reverse unfavorable decrees standing up against us, thwart demonic attacks, and massively rescue our souls, and our spirits from harm.

In their disposition, low-ranked angels can be subject to intimidation when faced with highly-ranked demonic spirits. These forces of darkness, due to the corrupt nature of our bloodline, take pleasure in being the police of curses and condemnations that existed way before our conception. Don't we read in Job 5? 7: *'For man is born for trouble, [As naturally] as sparks fly upward.'* Amplified Bible (AMP) These troubles are a natural blockade set to counter and resist salvation. Remember that this reality is first and foremost spiritual, and only spiritual forces can defeat or the least fight spiritual fights. To be in the fight, this is ineluctable, let alone winning it, is critical to have an understanding of the angels and their critical missions.

Essentially, the 5 missions identified by the French Naval Forces, are, in our sight, the main missions for the angels assigned to us. Help may be available, yet unused, for lack of understating. *Thank God for divine mercy in making us enjoy angelic support, regardless of our ignorance. Now, He is making it more manifest to us to request the help of this massive support system.*

By revelation, The Holy Spirit gives us understanding to grasp His primary mission: To glorify the Name of

Jesus, through signs and wonders. To go forth for The Light to shine. The Holy Spirit is the measure of God's Power endowed upon us, the very Power of God in action. Hence, He is not always set to intervene in our day-to-day activities, as His aim is to Glorify Jesus! Thus, the angels fulfill the call of assisting, helping, instructing, and even speaking on our behalf, daily.

To help us 'to give assistance or support to, to make more pleasant or bearable, to be of use to, to further the advancement of, to change for the better, to refrain from, to keep from occurring, to restrain (oneself) from doing something, to take something for (oneself) without permission, to give assistance or support, to be of use or benefit, etc...' according to Merriam-webster.com

To give assistance in doing what we are called to do, to receive support as we feel tired doing that which is what we are called to, is what angels are sent for. Heirs and heiresses to salvation can't do it by themselves. Consequently, assistance and support are not optional, but the very need we need to go after. In circumstances we cannot control, angels are to be of use to us, as they can take over, in order to further our advancement. Vashti occupied the Queen seat which, according to divine decree, was to be taken over by Esther. Angels made use of the King's drunkenness to further Esther's advancement in life, calling, destiny, etc... Through her advancement, the future of the Jews, under King Xerxes, changed for the better. Angels make this possible, Saints. From our addictions, iniquities, and wrongs, we are changed for the better, either saved or destined to be saved.

Have you experienced instances where you so long to commit adultery or fornication, yet have to deter thoughts, flashes, and reminders? As heirs and heiress of salvation, either an angel or the legion of angels lent you their power to refrain from such acts. Did you have suicidal thoughts, yet felt like giving yourself a second chance? Friend, you've just been refrained from harming yourself; in doubt? Think of the millions that die in the same act, unstopped, & render Glory to God. Yes, bless God for the redemption, as it's a sign amongst many that you are the heir or heiress of salvation.

Prayer: In Jesus' Name, we pray and declare angelic intervention in our battles against addictions, bad choices, deadly behaviors, and unholy acts. Let the angels of God help us refrain from doing that which can destroy our health, well-being, brains, lungs, and vital organs such as the circulatory, digestive, and respiratory systems in Jesus' Name.

We witnessed an accident that left us dumbfounded. No one, but God alone was able to rescue a mortal in such a way. A motorcyclist escaped a crash as a trailer totally smashed his engine. Right before our eyes, the moment the bike was being run over, it was as if a hand swiftly removed the sexagenarian from his seat and threw him inside the bush that bordered the highway. We were astonished; the survivor, first. How could one escape such a brutal hit? There was surely a mighty rescue operation sent forth to deliver a soul from the grave. His dismissal was kept from occurring, cries of mourning were prevented from taking over his house, and his funeral program was kept from being put together, a coffin prevented from making its way onto his perimeters. An angel rescued the man and kept the worst from occurring. Beloved, such is our situation, when we escape the worst.

To keep their evil plans, an angelic intervention was necessary to prolong the days of PeterMid-morning on that fateful day, he was en route to meet with his Boss, the minister of the interior and security. There on the bridge, was a man, lying down, profusely bleeding. The prefect of his region will order his chauffeur and bodyguard to stop the vehicle to lend a hand. Little did he know the rescued was on his way to eliminate him physically. Transported to the hospital, though in the coma, the wicked man would claim to be left alone, asking: 'Why should I kill him, why am I being bothered to kill Peter?' StunnPeterleft the hospital. An evil plan just got kept from occurring, a plan of destruction; a soul just got *redeemed from the pit* Psalms 103. 4

Prayer: We pray, in Jesus' Name, Father let your angels keep the worse from occurring. We command angels to keep our enemies from winning over us, hijacking our goods, and striking our health, peace, destinies, and finances in Jesus' Name.

Kingship was taken from the most robust and oldest son of Jessie without permission and given to David. Vashti was uncrowned and Esther received the crown without permission from anyone; that's what God's Angels do; to take things without permission for the good of heir and heiresses of salvation. What is yours by revelation, yet kept by a total stranger? Which perimeters are you called to possess, yet occupied by a usurper? What resources does the church need so dearly, yet find at the disposal of those who despise God's Name? We are to call on the Name of the Lord and request angelic support and in His mercy & Grace, angels will be given unto us for our good.

Prayer: In Jesus' Name, we pray the Lord to ennoble His chosen by angelic assistance in areas we know and ignore. Let the church, ministers, prophets, pastors, students, husbands, wives, men, women, the youth, graduates, professionals, the jobless, etc... be ennobled by angelic massive support.

The word 'help' also means, according to merriam-webster.com, to 'make more pleasant or bearable. Friends, heirs, and heiresses won't always experience greener pastures, but rather face some discomfort, trials, hardships, tribulations; yes, tribulations. 'Tribulation is defined as distress or suffering resulting from oppression or persecution... a trying experience' According to merriam-webster.com Jesus warned us consequently in John 16:33 *'I have told you these things, so that in Me you may have [perfect] peace. In the world, you have tribulation and distress and suffering, but be courageous [be confident, be undaunted, be filled with joy]; I have overcome the world.'* [My conquest is accomplished, My victory abiding.] [Amplified Bible (AMP)] Faced with the aforementioned circumstances, we need to take *'courage'*, to *'be confident'*, to *'be undaunted*, to *'be filled with joy'* and it happens that these state of mind or well-being aren't natural, but divine, and God's angels know best how to deploy them, apply them, and infuse them. What Christ means is contained within the very mission assigned to the angels: to help the mortals, the weak, the fleeting, and the 'material things' that we are.

Angels make our circumstances more pleasant or bearable, just because some of them are unpleasant or unbearable. When demonic forces strike us, the pains and hurts are sometimes unspeakable. Through divorces, business failures, and petty and humongous debts, the pain is unbearable. When someone is diagnosed with leukemia, failing kidneys, or the worst forms of cancer, yet can talk of the 'joy of the Lord'; angels have surely positioned themselves to make unpleasant situations more pleasant, unbearable pains, more bearable.

The end time ministers must bear in mind that, to prep you for greater purposes, great are your tribulations. No one can escape these facts of faith and God's perfect plans to train us, equip us, and use us. In the midst of the turmoil, if we can still claim that we 'are convinced that nothing can ever separate us from God's love' then God's angels are at work. Good news, we can ask for their deployment, more of them, as these beings are legions, many, plethoric We can then, cry it out louder: *'Neither death nor life, neither angels nor demons,[b] neither our fears for today nor our worries about tomorrow—not even the powers of hell can separate us from God's love. No power in the sky above or in the earth below—indeed, nothing in all creation will ever be able to separate us from the love of God that is revealed in Christ Jesus our Lord.'* Romans 8:38-39 [New Living Translation (NLT)]

We read in Psalm 81:7-8 [Complete Jewish Bible (CJB)] *"I lifted the load from his shoulder; his hands were freed from the [laborer's] basket. You called out when you were in trouble, and I rescued you; I answered you from the thundercloud; I tested you at the M'rivah Spring [by saying,]* (Selah). When God is testing heirs and heiresses, no rescue operation can be carried out, none, except when He allows the angels to *'lift the load from their shoulder'* and *'free them from the heavy basket.* Hence, the most, The Lord of Host, would do is to 'make the situation more pleasant, bearable. It's obvious God does test His chosen, as 'there are rivers to be crossed, mountains to be climbed', giants to arrest and keep bound; tasks ahead are too serious to let heirs and heiresses go untested.

We read on dictionary.cambridge.org test is 'an act of using something to find out if it is working correctly or how effective it is'; the example is indicative of what this is all about: 'The new missiles are currently undergoing tests.' Let's consider what a missile represents. On globalsecurity.org, we read: 'A Precision Guided Munitions [PGM] is a missile, bomb or artillery shell equipped with a terminal guidance system. It contains electrical equipment that guides it in the last phase before impact. The terminal guidance unit is designed to sense emitted or reflected EMR (electromagnetic radiation) within its field of view.' Without diving into much detail, heirs and heiresses are missiles, God chose to establish His Kingdom; God promised to put his Fire in our mouth, and a missile is nothing else but 'fire'. This material goes through tremendous stress to be compiled and set for use. Yes, our circumstances may look stressful, and terrible; such stress is necessary to let the host of witnesses (human and spiritual) know how effective we are. We get tested, each and every one of us, according to the measure of Grace given unto us.

To be tested, God uses contrary winds, misfortunes, and dark clouds. Those dark hours are a natural prescription for prayers. We cry, mourn, and confess. In the process, we feel isolated, not knowing that God wants us isolated from time to time for fellowship purposes. God is not always looking for our loud prayers, joyous dances, and all the 'spiritual frenzy', but a time with Him, where we listen to Him, not just us talking, asking, requesting, searching...During the testing, what His Angels do is to make things more bearable, and more pleasant. They remind us of the Glory ahead, and the faithfulness of God. Our spirits find comfort when reminded of God's goodness, and promises. Indeed, David said in Psalms 119. 50 *This is my comfort in my affliction, that your promise gives me life* [English Standard Version (ESV)] Affliction is defined as the cause of persistent pain or distress, 'great suffering' on merriam-webster.com. According to dictionary.com affliction means 'a cause of mental or bodily pain, as sickness, loss, calamity, or persecution.' These lines depict a terrible condition, a desperate situation David was in. We too, will go, at one point or the other in our walk with the Lord, to be chosen as heirs and heiresses. The reminder of God's promises to our spirit and soul will surely comfort us. Some of us might just experience Solomon's grace, with a father who fought all wars on his behalf.

Jesus went through a similar affliction as His days were drawing near to the end. A record shows He grieved so badly and his 'sweat became like great drops of blood falling down to the ground'. An angel was made available to make the situation more bearable, more pleasant, by '...*appearing to him... from heaven, strengthening him*'. We need strength to go through tribulations, and strength isn't always physical, but also emotional, internal, and moral. If Jesus needed strength and courage, then we who are co-heirs will surely need the help He received. Strength crowned with faith in the finished work of Christ Jesus!

To know and understand angelic ministration is key to enjoying their ministration to the fullest. A Head of a defense ministry, justice ministry, and finance ministry has to know their resources. A ministry of security won't and shouldn't deploy a military force to regulate traffic when the lights are off, as it's within the scope of the police forces.

THE HOLY SPIRIT, OVERSEER OF ALL SPIRITS

The Holy Spirit, God's Power in action, The Glory of Jesus, confers to the chosen ones, unction to function. Believers in Christ seek the unction to glorify Jesus, to speak in tongues, heal the sick, and bless the people. Subdued to the leading of the Holy Spirit, angels execute written judgments, favorable and unfavorable, decrees in time and space. Angels do not operate on their own, or on places of their choosing. Instructions are derived from spoken decisions, divine oracles, carried by the Holy Spirit. *'When the Spirit of truth comes, he will guide you into all the truth, for he will not speak on his own authority, but whatever he hears he will speak, and he will declare to you the things that are to come.'* John 16:13 [English Standard Version (ESV)] Angels, which are all under the command of The Holy Spirit, cannot go it alone, if the Commander Himself is subdued to another Authority, namely Christ Jesus. It has been as such since creation began. They are messengers, always 'SENT',"... Yet if there is an angel ... sent to ...," they are 'MESSENGERS'... If there's a messenger[o] appointed to mediate for Job..." Job 33.23 [International Standard Version]; hence they are SERVANTS, Representatives of God. That's why it's wrong to adore, praise, and venerate angels, as these beings hold nothing that warrants praise from us; all they do is serve, defend, and its corollary. I rest assured that appreciation unto them could be God's affair, not us; after all, no scriptures suggest worshipping and/or praising them. The last time someone prostrated before an angel of God, he was rebuked sharply by the latter.

The Holy Spirit is simply God's Power in action, God's Authority manifest, & the Glory of Christ deployed. Many passages in the Scriptures have an account of this fact: *'Now it is God who makes both us and you stand firm in Christ. He anointed us, set his seal of ownership on us, and put his Spirit in our hearts as a deposit, guaranteeing what is to come.'* 2 Corinthians 21-22 [New International Version (NIV)]. In Acts 16:7, we read: *'Then coming to the borders of Mysia, they headed north for the province of Bithynia, but again the Spirit of Jesus did not allow them to go there.'* [New Living Translation] *'...for I know that through your prayers and the help of the Spirit of Jesus*

Christ, this will turn out for my deliverance...' Philippians 1:19 [English Standard Version]

It's critical to establish the strategic rapport between humans and the Holy Spirit and humans and the angels of God.

The Holy Spirit and us

We are made the Temple of God, by divine grace. Physical buildings aren't the church of the New Testament, but the body of Christ. Hence, the Holy Spirit doesn't inhabit concrete walls, but the people. If we are God's properties, then, His Glory will shine upon us. There are temples that grab attention, mind-provoking; one may ask what the inside could look like. There is a glory manifest. When physical temples are referred to, one may think of the biggest and largest basilica of the world, located in Cote d'Ivoire, and the Full Gospel Church of Seoul, pastored by David Yonggi Cho. Indeed, these temples carry an 'absolute glory' in the sight of men. You can't escape their massive appearance, their splendid look. One can't talk of beautiful buildings without their designers in mind. Architects are referred to in a respectful way when buildings are erected according to their genius design. Talk of these 2 temples in honorable, reverential manners and you'll be showing great admiration to their designers. That which catches the sight is the glory upon these buildings and the Glory is brought about by virtue of the creative 'spirit' of the designers, the architects. Similarly, that which glories the Temples that we are, is the 'CREATIVE SPIRIT' of God.

God's spirit, the Holy Spirit is He Who glories God's Name, God's properties. John 16:14 stipulates: *"He will glorify me, for he will take what is mine and declare it to you."* [English Standard Version]

What's glory? Dictionary.com reads "very great praise, honor, or distinction bestowed by common consent, something that is a source of honor, fame, or admiration; a distinguished ornament or an object of pride, adoring praise or worshipful thanksgiving, a state of great splendor, magnificence, or prosperity, a state of absolute happiness, gratification, contentment, the splendor and bliss of heaven." It adds: "a ring, circle, or surrounding radiance of light represented about the head or the whole figure of a sacred person, as Christ or a saint"

Many believers around the world give very great praise and honor to the Name of Jesus, thanks to the Holy Spirit. Multitudes render worshipful thanksgiving and adoring praise every second, hour, and day. This is done through the deployed magnificence upon that Name, the Name of Jesus. It's written somewhere: '*The heavens declare the glory of God, and the firmament shows his handiwork.*' Psalm 19. 1 [American Standard Version (ASV)] One can't look at the heavens and not be amazed. Camera photos click profusely when unique patterns display up in the sky; the clouds get pretty fancy at times, and that's simply GLORY. Be a believer or a so-called atheist, no one resists the constant Glory carried out by Heaven. Besides, we, as Temples of The Holy Ghost have a rare privilege to shine, to bear the splendor and bliss of heaven. Israel Houghton sang it right by asserting: 'Your Presence is Heaven To Me', indeed. When deployed, The Holy Spirit serves one purpose: To Glorify the Name of Jesus, The Name of God. The Holy Spirit is the deployment of 'great beauty and splendor' [merriam-webster.com]. The Holy Spirit marks us with beauty and resplendence.

Inhabited by the Spirit of God, we're turned into a state of great splendor, and magnificence, and consequently, the endgame is to make us prosper in all respect. Scriptures give an account of God's Glory in Genesis 12:14-15: 'And when Abram entered Egypt, the Egyptians saw that Sarai was very beautiful. Pharaoh's princes (officials) also saw her and praised her to Pharaoh, and the woman was taken [for the purpose of marriage] into Pharaoh's house (harem)'. [Amplified Bible (AMP)] One may argue that this passage refers to physical and natural beauty which isn't totally accurate. By divine illumination, we are able to assert that this was a spiritual Glory that befell Sarah. Not all the beautiful ladies, foreigners, and domestic were brought to the King; moreover, Egypt had super cute females throughout the kingdom. Sara could have been a beautiful woman in the land of Abraham, but surely one amongst a multitude God's spirit made her splendid to fulfill a purpose. We are made splendid, regardless of our physical insufficiencies, to fulfill a purpose. *'When Moses came down from Mount Sinai with the two tablets of the Testimony in his hand, he did not know that the skin of his face was shining [with a unique radiance] because he had been speaking with God. When Aaron and all the Israelites saw Moses, behold, the skin of his face shone, and they were afraid to approach him. But Moses called to them, and Aaron and all the leaders of the congregation returned to him; and he spoke to them. Afterward all the Israelites approached him, and he commanded them to do everything that the Lord had said to him on Mount Sinai.'* Exodus 34:29-33 [Amplified Bible (AMP)] There was surely a purpose for the Glory Moses bore. Pleading with God for such a transformation isn't an option of the church, but a calling. Lacking in this dimension harms us tremendously, eliminates our testimonies, and asserts our nonentity. Evil spirits laugh at us when we lack in this Glory. Many are God's servants who lack this gift. They pray for the sick and the condition of the latter gets worse than it was initially; others ask for healing, blessings, etc. upon the flock and God's glory is shown. This glory isn't for the leaders only but for God's church.

Let's not overlook the importance of the Spirit within us and upon us. God's glory can be upon a medium to heal, just like Christ Jesus spat on a sand to heal the blind recover sights, or Paul's handkerchief that heals the sick. We hear men and women of God assert that: 'the Spirit descends upon me and I began to prophesy, heal...' Archbishop Duncan William declared on one occasion that, though he's not a Prophet, the prophetic anointing descended upon him to declare God's plan to make Olusegun Obasanjo the next President of Nigerian after a political transition took place; a word deemed crazy by those in attendance, including the clergy. The man is inhabited by the Holy Spirit, yet the prophetic mantle descended upon him to proclaim the oracles of God. We may call it a 'prompt' or 'punctual' anointing, Glory. This doesn't just occur to believers but means or resources of God's own choosing. Even a donkey had that Glory once, as the beast spoke in the human tongue to instill wisdom in men. We've heard instances where prostitutes, drunkards, and unsavory entities bore the same splendor, but again, for a short time, and for a purpose.

We need God's glory every day, every hour, every minute, and every second. God's glory keeps away demonic princes and spirits, and guarantees us safety and massive divine support, up in the air, down on earth, and below. Jesus shed tears resembling blood when the hour came for the Glory to depart from HIM for the purpose of dying for us. Jesus deplored such a state deeply, to the point of asking the Heavenly Father to review His decision if possible, sort of: let the Glory not depart, yet I'm willing to die. He'll quickly realize that the Glory will suffocate the prophecy from being fulfilled. The Anointing, the Holy Spirit upon and in Him will surely defeat his death on the cross, literally, and physically. The Death on the Cross wouldn't have been possible. The Anointing, God's Glory makes it almost impossible for demonic plans to succeed. We assert 'almost impossible' for the fulfillment of the prophecy because while Jesus was still pleading, God's Glory hadn't yet departed from him, yet the prophecy was triggered. A temple may go through upgrade mode, which could equal trials, tribulations, discomfort, great pains, long-suffering, and afflictions; however, the Glory is still there. Should Christ benefit from the fullness of God's Glory, the Only Man that ever enjoyed such a state, those who accused and touched HIM in a harmful way would have caused God's wrath, and drawn a fierce Angelic Intervention or the whole passion prophecy won't have even started. By divine illumination, we are able to assert that God's Glory is for God; to Caesar what belongs to him, and to God, His own matchless 'stuff. God is right to warn spirits and living beings in these paraphrased terms: *'My glory, I won't share, do not touch, and play with it' Isaiah 42:8 The Holy Spirit is primarily, God's Power & Beauty in men and serves God's own purposes. In doubt? When Christ triumphantly entered Jerusalem, the Glory of God was shown in the full sight of everyone in attendance. Scriptures say: "And they bring the colt to Jesus. And they throw their cloaks on it, and He sat on it. And many spread their cloaks on the road. And others spread leafy branches, having cut them from the fields. And the ones going ahead and the ones following were crying out Hosanna!' Blessed is the One coming in the name of the Lord. Blessed is the coming kingdom of our Father David. Hosanna in the highest [heavens]!'* Mark ii. 7-10 [Disciples' Literal New Testament (DLNT)]. Christ being our Lord, rides in on us, and Glory moves people to spread their cloaks, praising God as we manifest, heal the sick, bless the poor, and preach the Gospel with signs and wonders, yet the cloaks and leafy branches we walk upon, the Glory upon the donkey doesn't belong to the donkey, but the one riding in on the donkey. That's who we are, all of us who operate under the Anointing, the reflection of God's glory. Heirs and heiresses are given honor, by reason of the Crown, represented by the King. Consequently, the Holy Spirit is God's Spirit and carries His Glory 24/7; visibly/ invisibly or in subtle/ manifest ways in time and space; however, God's Glory moves angels to show up and minister to us.

Prayer: Father I'm the temple of your Spirit, the temple of your Glory and Manifestation, make me splendid, resplendent, and in your image. Just like magnificent buildings are identified by their designers, let nations identify me by your Glory upon me, your presence upon and in me to fulfill that which you've shown me grace and mercy in making me part of your creation in Jesus' Mighty Name.

The Angels and us

When a building is erected, it needs a support system to stand, stay clean, and be well-kept. Nice-looking buildings, temples especially, need absolute housekeeping, janitors, maintenance, and a security apparatus to ever be secured, maintained, and keep their glories. God's Glory gives glory, indeed.

On en.oxforddictionaries.com we read: "The Temple either of two successive religious buildings of the Jews in Jerusalem. The first (957–586 BC) was built by Solomon and destroyed by Nebuchadnezzar; it contained the Ark of the Covenant. The second (515 BC–AD 70) was enlarged by Herod the Great in 20 BC and destroyed by the Romans during a Jewish revolt; all that remains is the Wailing Wall., A place of Christian public worship " From the outset, it stands to point out that temples can be destroyed, rebuilt, and destroyed again; so are we.

Scriptures give an account of the splendor of the successive temples, especially the first one. Special stuff needs special coverage, maintenance, and security. Let's look into the basic services a temple needs.

Maintaining a building requires a panoply of tasks. Come to think of it. Security forces, housekeeping services, and a plethora of other positions need not be vacant.

Please note that all these tasks can only be performed by workers and experts; these are the angels and their ministries. In the US, the government cabinet members are called 'Secretaries'; however, elsewhere in the world, these positions are called: Ministries. Does that sound a bit indicative to us?

Again, Hebrews 1. 14 asserted: *'Are they, not all ministering spirits, sent forth to minister for those who shall be heirs of salvation?'* [21st Century King James Version (KJ21)]. If we are a kingdom, then we've got a business to handle. A government is made of Ministers, whose roles are to minister. To underestimate their functions and impacts is to make one's state of affairs chaotic, anarchistic, and utterly dangerous. What's then a government ministry?

Dictionary.com offers insights into the meaning of the word ministry. It's " the service, functions, or profession of a minister of religion, the body or class of ministers of religion; clergy, the service, function, or office of a minister of state, the body of ministers of state, (usually initial capital letter) any of the administrative governmental departments of certain countries usually under the direction of a minister of state, (usually initial capital letter) the building that houses such an administrative department, the term of office of a minister of state" These specifics depict the relevancy of the angelic ministry which is destined to make our lives much easier.

In some state governments, we have as many as 40 to 50 ministers, secretaries, or undersecretaries. Without boring us with their attributes and prerogatives, let's remind ourselves that for a nation to run its affairs smoothly, these helpers are needed on a daily basis, running from big to little details. The Ministry of Health must function, not only to cure existing ailments but prevent new ones. Police forces must keep the cities and their streets drug-free, crime-free, anarchy-free, and money laundering which affects negatively the Internal Revenue, sexual slavery, and slavery in all forms, and prevent organized terror gathering and reinforcements. The defense military must keep the borders of our perimeters safe and secured, our gates and doorposts sealed, and unbreakable, new strategies and resources are to be developed, acquired, and set to counter every breach by stronger foes. The Justice Ministry must reverse unfavorable verdicts from within or out and favor their own citizens, cancel extradition decrees deemed to harm their citizens, and render justice to the widow, the orphans, the poor, etc... The Agriculture Ministry must find ways to prosper its citizens and help feed them with fresh grains, quality crops, etc... What about the huge responsibilities the Economy & Finance Ministry ought to bear to ensure the nation is never in a delinquent state? Now, Imagine for a second, a nation that has no government. How pertinent is it to know, understand, and enjoy angelic ministry? That's the point of reading these lines and I hope it profits you beyond your wildest imagination, according to God's infinite favor and mercy in Jesus Name!

From the prevention of loss of loved ones to our jobs, memory, etc. it's awesome to see God's own intelligent way to support his people destined to salvation every day. They may be invisible, but countless angels and archangels are at your service.

Isn't God Almighty too gracious, merciful and loving unconditionally?

REFERENCES

- https://wwz.ifremer.fr/L-ocean-pour-tous/Comprendre-les-oceans
- https://www.militaryfactory.com/ranks/index.asp
- https://www.navy.com/about.html
- http://www.fondationdelamer.org/barometre/
- http://coldcasechristianity.com/2014/seven-important-differences-between-angels-and-demons/
- https://www.hymnal.net/en/hymn/h/789
- http://www.haaretz.com/middle-east-news/1.813202